GW00363209

THE
GARDEN
POCKET PUZZLE
BOOK

DAVID SQUIRE

summersdale

THE GARDEN POCKET PUZZLE BOOK

This edition published in 2015 by Summersdale Publishers Ltd.

First published by Summersdale Publishers Ltd in 2012

Copyright © David Squire, 2012

Summersdale Publishers Ltd
46 West Street
Chichester
West Sussex
PO19 1RP
UK

www.summersdale.com

Printed and bound in the Czech Republic

ISBN: 978-1-84953-682-0

Substantial discounts on bulk quantities of Summersdale books are available to corporations, professional associations and other organisations. For details contact Nicky Douglas by telephone: +44 (0) 1243 756902, fax: +44 (0) 1243 786300 or email: nicky@summersdale.com.

PREFACE

My enthusiasm for plants and growing them has been with me for many years, even before I studied at the Hertfordshire College of Horticulture and as a student at the Royal Horticultural Society's Garden at Wisley, Surrey. Similar to all hobbies, the more one 'gardens' the greater the interest for this all-embracing pastime. For me it has broadened into a passion for collecting facts about plants and the folklore woven around them. These encompass the selection of a marriage partner, marriage, illness, death and country cures, as well as the many annual village festivities popular several centuries ago, and which often left a legacy for today. This, the first of my puzzle books, provides many hours of amusement when you are not active in your garden. It is a near-endless source of amusement and brain-teasing – ideal for armchair gardening or when retreating to a potting shed during a spell of wet weather.

David Squire

ABOUT THE PUZZLES

These varied and mind-questioning puzzles include the following types. Some are word puzzles and some are 'spidermite crosswords'; others involve mixtures of letters and are known as 'jumbleys'. Here is an insight into the range of puzzles you will find in this book:

• SPIDERMITE CROSSWORDS
Form simple frameworks using the words listed.

• WORDSEARCH PUZZLES
Spotting words in a seemingly random medley of letters can stretch the mind!

• SPOT THE DIFFERENCE
Fun pages where you are asked to find the differences between two pictures.

• JUMBLEYS
Mixtures of letters that can be reassembled to form the names of well-known plants and flowers.

• REBUS PUZZLES
These puzzles are formed of letters and pictures which together make up the names of plants.

• PAIRING UP

Matching common names with botanical names is just one form of 'pairing up' puzzle.

• POTPOURRI PUZZLES

Wide and varied, but they all show how the histories of plants, gardens and people are interwoven and form part of our garden and countryside heritage. These range from witchcraft protection and fertility solutions to superstitions about ageing and searching for a lover.

• FLOWERS AND PLANTS IN LITERATURE

Poetry and verse are steeped in references to plants and flowers and you will no doubt remember many of them.

• GARDENING QUOTATIONS AND PROVERBS

These have always been a popular way to foresee the many happenings in a gardener's calendar, and they encompass weather, sowing and harvesting predictions.

• GREEN GARDENING

Keeping clear of garden chemicals is important for gardeners, and many puzzles focus on green husbandry to keep plants healthy. These range from controlling greenfly to deterring carrot rootflies and moles.

The answers to these challenging puzzles are to be found at the end of the book.

1

PAIRING UP

Here are the jumbled-up names of six popular culinary herbs. Can you pair them up correctly and then add the common names?

Anethum	carvi
Anthriscus	didyma
Carum	graveolens
Glycyrrhiza	officinalis
Melissa	cerefolium
Monarda	glabra

◇

2

ROSE JUMBLEY

Many rose varieties have an ancient pedigree. Which variety, introduced in 1868, is hidden in the following letters?

QACUESJ RATIERC

3

FLOWERS IN LITERATURE

Who wrote the following?

'What's in a name? That which we call a rose
By any other word would smell as sweet.'

- Alfred, Lord Tennyson
- Charles Lamb
- Christopher Marlowe
- Geoffrey Chaucer
- William Shakespeare

—◇—

4

SHRUB REBUS

Try making out the botanical name for the Sea Buckthorn, sometimes known as Sallow Thorn. A clue is given below.

 PHAE   NOIDES

5

COMMON NAME CONUNDRUM

Some countryside plants abound in common names.
To which viola do all of these names refer?

Kiss-me-quick, Cat's Face, Biddy's Eyes, Love-in-vain,
Lover's Thoughts, Lover-and-idle and Kiss-behind-the-
garden-gate.

---◇---

6

BAD LUCK AND
GOOD LUCK PLANTS

Many plants are thought to bring luck, while others have
a darker side. Most of the following plants bring good
fortune, but which are the ones you would not trust?

1. Artemisia
2. Cherry blossom
3. Cherry tree
4. Four-leaved clover
5. Elder
6. Hawthorn (indoors)
7. Hawthorn (outdoors)
8. Lavender
9. Rosemary
10. White heather

7

UNUSUAL FRAGRANCE

Which of these plants has the common name
Cherry Pie on account of its flowers producing a heavy
and fruity fragrance?

- *Convallaria majalis*
- *Heliotropium arborescens*
- *Iris pumila*
- *Lilium auratum*
- *Monarda didyma*

---◇---

8

THE CRYSTAL PALACE

The Great Exhibition of 1851 was held in a glass and
cast-iron exhibition hall erected in Hyde Park, London.
It became known as the Crystal Palace – but who gave
it this name?

- *News of the World*
- *Punch*
- *The Daily Telegraph*
- *The Penge Gazette*
- *The Times*

9
CULINARY HERB WORDSEARCH

- Alecost
- Angelica
- Aniseed
- Balm
- Basil
- Bay
- Bergamot
- Borage
- Caraway
- Chervil
- Chives
- Coriander
- Dill
- Fennel

- Garlic
- Ginger
- Horseradish
- Hyssop
- Liquorice
- Lovage
- Marjoram
- Mint
- Rosemary
- Rue
- Sage
- Sorrel
- Tansy
- Thyme

A	T	H	Y	M	E	X	P	L	V	C	S	D	S	A
N	N	A	S	C	C	Z	O	I	D	K	L	G	N	V
I	I	W	N	E	G	A	S	V	J	H	F	G	L	B
S	M	E	G	S	V	V	S	R	U	E	E	A	I	H
E	R	T	R	B	Y	I	Y	E	G	L	N	R	Q	S
E	E	F	G	H	J	B	H	H	I	O	N	L	U	I
D	D	Y	A	W	A	R	A	C	F	V	E	I	O	D
Y	N	L	Y	E	L	S	A	A	P	A	L	C	R	A
R	A	E	H	J	Q	S	E	T	B	G	J	N	I	R
E	I	R	S	D	K	G	E	C	S	E	G	H	C	E
G	R	R	A	L	A	G	L	L	V	O	R	P	E	S
N	O	O	I	R	V	B	N	M	N	Z	C	B	D	R
I	C	S	O	R	O	S	E	M	A	R	Y	E	I	O
G	A	B	A	Y	M	A	R	J	O	R	A	M	L	H
B	A	L	M	B	E	R	G	A	M	O	T	S	L	A

10

EMPRESS JOSÉPHINE

Which plant did the Empress Joséphine popularize throughout Europe in the early 1800s, becoming so widely grown that it was claimed to be a characteristic of London in the same way that the redolence of freshly roasted coffee was known in Paris? Was it:

- African Marigold
- Dahlia
- French Marigold
- Mignonette

11

WEATHER-FORECASTING FLOWER

Which flower is known as Poor Man's Weather-glass and Scarlet Pimpernel because its scarlet flowers usually open about 8 am and close about 3 pm?

- *Anagallis arvensis*
- *Bellis perennis*
- *Primula vulgaris*

12
BOTANIC GARDENS

Many early botanic gardens were founded in Europe, but when were they created in Britain? Can you date these three:

- Cambridge Botanic Garden
- Chelsea Physic Garden
- Oxford Botanic Garden

13
WALL SHRUB JUMBLEY

Which popular wall shrub with coloured berries is formed from these letters?

ANTHARACPY

14

ANNUAL FLOWER JUMBLEY

With masses of yellow-centred white flowers, this annual
creates a spectacular display. Which one is it?

DEHCAOP GEG WERFLO

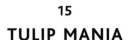

15

TULIP MANIA

When did tulip mania rage in Holland?

- 1520 to 1542
- 1634 to 1637
- 1645 to 1648

16

EARLY GRAFTING

Grafting plants – the unification of a rooted part
and desired variety – has been carried out for
hundreds of years.

Here are a few grafting tools popular in the
16th century – can you name them?

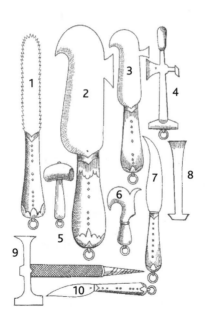

17
FLOWER SONG

Which flower featured in a song in the 1965 film
The Sound of Music?

- Alpine Willow Herb
- Blue-eyed Mary
- Cyclamen
- Edelweiss

18
CONIFER JUMBLEY

A well-known stately conifer with spreading
branches is hidden in these letters.

DEARC FO NONBAEL

19

HERB JUMBLEY

With other common names, such as Mace and Costmary, the leaves of this culinary herb have been used to flavour ales. Which one is it?

TSOCLEA

---◇---

20

CHAUCER'S TIME CLOCK

Which plant did Geoffrey Chaucer (1340–1400) call Day's Eye on account of its flowers opening in the morning when the sun shines and closing in the afternoon?

- Daisy
- Forget-me-not
- Meadow Cranesbill
- Stinking Mayweed

21
SPOT THE DIFFERENCE

Below is a well-known illustration from Peter Treveris's
Grete Herball, published in 1526 and again in 1529 (it
was mainly a translation from *Le Grant Herbier*, a French
publication). It shows the harvesting of grapes and is a
superb example of early book illustration. Although
mainly shown in outline form, with slight shading, this
illustration reveals an aspect of gardening in the
16th century.

Grapes are being harvested and placed in a wicker basket
for taking to a winery. There are also plants growing
in a basket container, together with naked but modest
decorative figures.

On the left is a reproduction of the original illustration.
Can you spot ten differences in the version shown below?

22
PAIN-EASING HERBS

Many plants are famed for their ability to ease pain.
Out of the following ten herbs, which two do not have
pain-easing qualities?

1. Black Cohosh
2. Californian Poppy
3. Cherry Laurel
4. Cloves
5. Evening Primrose
6. Goutweed
7. Guelder Rose
8. Herb Christopher
9. Monkey Flower
10. Toothwort

◇

23
GRAVES OF INNOCENT PEOPLE

Which flower was said to thrive on graves of
innocent people?

• Rosemary
• Rose
• White Lily

24
FLOWER-SELLER CRIES

Many street flower-sellers during the 1600s and later had songs specially associated with their wares. Can you complete the following traditional London street cry:

'Who'll buy my lavender, fresh lavender…'

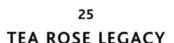

25
TEA ROSE LEGACY

In 1870, the Tea Rose 'Lady Hillingdon' was introduced by the nursery of Lowe and Shawyer at Hillingdon, a few miles west of London. It became the largest cut-flower nursery in the world – but who occupies the site now?

26

INEBRIATE SOLUTION

One popular plant is claimed to prevent a drunkard from
drinking, but which one?

- Gorse
- Holly
- Privet
- White Heather

---◇---

27

WITCHCRAFT PROTECTION

When planted near a front door, this shrub has been
claimed to prevent the entry of witches. It is also a plant
of remembrance. Which of these is it:

- Gorse
- Heather
- Pyracantha
- Rosemary

28

PAIRING UP

Try pairing up the botanical and common names of these six popular conifers:

Araucaria araucana	Maidenhair Tree
Calocedrus decurrens	Italian Cypress
Cedrus atlantica	English Yew
Cupressus sempervirens	Incense Cedar
Ginkgo biloba	Monkey Puzzle
Taxus baccata	Atlas Cedar

———◇———

29

APPLE JUMBLEY

This popular apple was introduced in 1876 and soon became a well-known culinary variety.

RAMBYEL'S SINGELED

TEA ROSE REDOLENCE

Identifying the redolence of Tea Roses has puzzled many rosarians. Does it have the smell of:

- A freshly opened packet of tea (but not tarry Lapsang)
- Powdered tea bags
- Stale brewed tea

AGEING SUPERSTITION

Carrying a nut in your pocket is claimed to prevent ageing.

Which one of the following nuts will keep you young?

- Acorn
- Chestnut
- Cobnut
- Walnut

32

WOUND-HEALING HERBS

Some herbs have a history of being used to heal wounds. Out of the following ten herbs, which two were not used to heal wounds?

1. Bugle
2. Cocklebur
3. Comfrey
4. Daisy
5. Dandelion

6. Hedge Garlic
7. Leopard's Bane
8. Medlar
9. Ploughman's Spikenard
10. Sphagnum Moss

———◇———

33

VEGETABLE ACCIDENTS

One vegetable is said to have seeds that contain souls of the dead, and when its plants are in flower accidents are likely to happen, but which one?

- Broad beans
- French beans
- Garden peas
- Runner beans

GARDEN PEST
SPIDERMITE CROSSWORD

Gardens, with their clusters of succulent plants waiting to be sucked, chewed and eaten, are oases of pleasure for insects. Here are twenty garden pests; how many can you find in the spidermite crossword on the opposite page? We have added eight key letters to help you.

• Birds	• Leafminer
• Blackfly	• Leatherjackets
• Caterpillars	• Millipedes
• Cockchafers	• Onion fly
• Earwigs	• Pea thrip
• Eelworms	• Raspberry moth
• Flea beetles	• Slugs
• Froghoppers	• Snails
• Greenfly	• Vine weevils
• Leafhoppers	• Woodlice

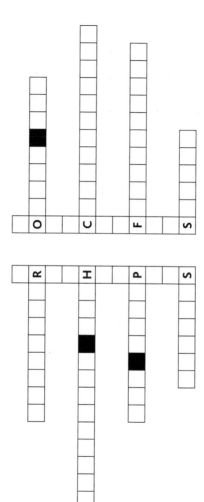

35
GOOD LUCK VEGETABLE

As well as creating claimed invisibility, the root of one
vegetable is also said to bring good luck, but which one?

- Beetroot
- Carrot
- Chicory
- Parsnip

36
RHEUMATISM PROTECTION

With this nut in your pocket, you are said to be given
protection from rheumatism, but which one?

- Acorn
- Nutmeg
- Peanut
- Walnut

37
PLUM JUMBLEY

This is one of the most widely grown plum varieties,
ideal for both culinary and dessert purposes.

COTRIVIA

38
CHERRY JUMBLEY

Popular, heavy-cropping, sweet-fruited cherry variety
with pale yellow skin that is flushed dark red. Can you
identify it from the following jumbled-up letters?

POLEONNA GARRIBEAU

39
PAIRING UP

Try pairing up the botanical names of these
water garden plants.

Aponogeton	*crassipes*
Butomus	*distachyos*
Calla	*aquaticum*
Eichhornia	*palustris*
Hottonia	*umbellatus*
Orontium	*palustris*

---◇---

40
PEAR JUMBLEY

This is one of the best-known dessert pear varieties.

OERECEFCNN

41
PAIRING UP

Bromeliads are fascinating houseplants, with attractive leaves sometimes forming urn-like centres. Here are six popular examples – try pairing up the common and botanical names.

Blushing Bromeliad	*Cryptanthus zonatus*
Coral Berry	*Billbergia nutans*
Pheasant Leaf	*Neoregelia carolinae*
Queen's Tears	*Ananas bracteatus*
Red Pineapple	*Aechmea fulgens*
Zebra Plant	*Cryptanthus fosterianus*

42
GARDENING QUOTATION

How does this continue?

'The best place to seek God is in a garden...'

43
PAIRING UP

Succulent houseplants are related to cacti (but do not have spines, short hooks or woolly hairs growing on them). Here are six popular succulent plants – try pairing up the common and botanical names.

Devil's Backbone	*Cotyledon orbiculata*
Panda Bear	*Faucaria tigrina*
Partridge-breasted Aloe	*Kalanchoe daigremontiana*
Pearl Plant	*Aloe variegata*
Pig's Ears	*Kalanchoe tomentosa*
Tiger Jaws	*Haworthia margarifera*

44
GARDENING QUOTATION

How does this continue?

'God made rainy days so that gardeners could ...'

45

KNOW YOUR ONIONS!

Vegetables are usually known by their common names,
but they do have botanical ones. Here is a medley of them
– can you link them to the correct vegetable?

1. *Allium cepa*
2. *Asparagus officinalis*
3. *Beta vulgaris*
4. *Brassica oleracea*
5. *Capsicum annuum*
6. *Capsicum frutescens*
7. *Cichorium endiva*
8. *Cichorium intybus*
9. *Daucus carota*
10. *Lactuca sativa*

11. *Lotus tetragonolobus*
12. *Lycopersicon esculentum*
13. *Phaseolus coccineus*
14. *Phaseolus vulgaris*
15. *Pisum sativum*
16. *Raphanus sativus*
17. *Solanum melongena*
18. *Solanum tuberosum*
19. *Vicia faba*
20. *Zea mays*

46
PAIRING UP

Indoor ferns have been popular since the Victorian era.
Try pairing up the common and botanical names of
these ones.

Bird's Nest Fern	*Asplenium bulbiferum*
Button Fern	*Pteris cretica*
Hen-and-Chickens Fern	*Pellaea rotundifolia*
Maidenhair Fern	*Platycerium bifurcatum*
Staghorn Fern	*Asplenium nidus*
Table Fern	*Adiantum raddianum*

———◇———

47
CROP VALUE FORECASTS

Some weather predictions foretold the value of crops.
Can you complete the following saying?

'If it freezes on St Thomas's Day,
The price of ...'

48

FRUIT JUMBLEY

This fruit has loganberries, blackberries and raspberries in
its parentage. Can you identify it?

SERRYBENYOB

49

ROYAL ASSOCIATION

Young shoot tips and flowers of this wild plant can be
boiled and eaten with butter. Its botanical name is
Chenopodium bonus-henricus, but what is its
common name?

- Charlock
- Dittander
- Good King Henry
- Red Campion
- Sea Kale

GARDEN DISEASE WORDSEARCH

These are usually less obvious than pests, but equally dangerous. Here are a few of them – how many can you find?

• Clubroot	• Leaf roll virus
• Cluster cup rust	• Peach leaf curl
• Coral spot	• Potato scab
• Damping-off	• Potato wart
• Dieback	• Powdery mildew
• Downy mildew	• Rot
• Fairy ring	• Rust
• Foot rot	• Scab
• Fusarium wilt	• Sooty mould
• Grey mould	• Tulip virus
• Honey fungus	• Wilt

A	F	D	A	M	P	I	N	G	O	F	F	C	S	P
C	E	U	O	F	I	W	H	T	Y	B	A	O	U	E
W	L	Z	S	W	G	L	S	C	T	K	I	R	R	A
X	E	U	N	A	N	U	D	K	L	C	R	A	I	C
M	S	D	S	D	R	Y	V	E	I	A	Y	L	V	H
B	O	U	L	T	S	I	M	L	W	B	R	S	L	L
A	O	G	G	I	E	U	U	I	U	E	I	P	L	E
C	T	C	R	N	M	R	R	M	L	I	N	O	O	A
S	Y	F	L	E	U	Y	C	I	W	D	G	T	R	F
O	M	O	E	U	Y	F	R	U	V	I	E	T	F	C
T	O	O	S	C	B	M	Y	E	P	P	L	W	A	U
A	U	T	V	C	F	R	O	E	D	R	I	T	E	R
T	L	R	O	T	A	I	O	U	N	W	U	L	L	L
O	D	O	W	H	Z	B	G	O	L	O	O	S	U	S
P	O	T	A	T	O	W	A	R	T	D	H	P	T	T

51
VALENTINE'S DAY RHYME

Can you complete the following lover's rhyme?

'The rose is red, the violet's blue,
Pinks are ...'

———————◇———————

52
WEATHER RHYME

There are many agricultural weather rhymes.
Can you complete the following?

'When the cuckoo comes to the bare thorn,
Sell your cow and buy your corn;
But when ...'

53
PAIRING UP

Cacti are popular houseplants and ideal for placing on windowsills. Here are six popular ones – try pairing up the common and botanical names.

Bishop's Cap Cactus	*Cephalocereus senilis*
Bunny's Ears	*Aporocactus flagelliformis*
Old Man Cactus	*Astrophytum myriostigma*
Peanut Cactus	*Cleistocactus strausii*
Rat's Tail Cactus	*Chamaecereus silvestrii*
Silver Torch Cactus	*Opuntia microdasys*

―――――◇―――――

54
GARDENING QUOTATION

How does this end?

'How fair is a garden amid the trials ...'

55

PAIRING UP

Palms introduce stateliness to conservatories and rooms
indoors. Try pairing up the common and botanical names
of these well-known examples.

Howea forsteriana	Bamboo Palm
Chamaerops humilis	Belmore Sentry Palm
Howea belmoreana	Dwarf Fan Palm
Rhapis excelsa	Fishtail Palm
Caryota mitis	Kentia Palm

---◇---

56

GARDENING QUOTATION

How does this end?

'Our England is a garden, and such gardens are not
made by singing ...'

57
HERB REBUS

This culinary herb may appear to have been sent from heaven. Can you name it?

ICA

58
CANTERBURY TALES

Written by Geoffrey Chaucer, the Father of English Literature, *The Canterbury Tales* encompasses stories from several people. Can you identify three of them that are also famous New English Roses?

- The Bouncer
- The Hayward
- The Prioress
- The Reeve
- The Squire

59
PAIRING UP

Insectivorous plants are fascinating and many can be grown indoors as houseplants. Try pairing up the common and botanical names of these popular plants.

Common Butterwort	*Drosera binata*
Forked-leaved Sundew	*Pinguicula vulgaris*
Hooded Pitcher Plant	*Sarracenia flava*
Purple Pitcher Plant	*Darlingtonia californica*
Venus Fly Trap	*Sarracenia purpurea*
Yellow Trumpet	*Dionaea muscipula*

60
GARDENING PROVERB

From which European country does the following proverb originate?

'The garden is the poor man's apothecary.'

61

FLOWERS IN SONGS

Who wrote this, and can you complete the second line?

'Roses are shining in Picardy,
In the hush of ...'

62

WHICH FRUIT?

There are many country names for soft fruits,
but to which one do all of these refer?

- Carberry
- Dewberry
- Groser
- Grozzle
- Honey-blob
- Peaberry

63
GARDENING PROVERB

How does this continue?

'Love is not like a potato. You cannot ...'

64
HERBACEOUS REBUS

Herbaceous perennial with leaves copied in classical
architecture. Can you name it?

AC  HUS

65

MOON SEED-SOWING

During earlier centuries, the phases of the moon were taken to indicate successful seed-sowing times. Can you complete the following rhyme?

'Sow peasen and beans in the wane of the moon,
Who soweth them sooner, he soweth too soon,
That they ...'

66

MAKING HAY!

The range of weather rhymes is very wide and includes harvest forecasts. Can you complete this one?

'A wet May makes ...'

67

SPOT THE DIFFERENCE

Farming in the 15th century was robust and usually included the majority of village members. It was also dangerous, with little thought for health and safety and undertaking 'risk assessment'. Non-complying villagers could find themselves in the stocks.

The original illustration (opposite) is taken from *Farming in the Middle Ages*. There are ten differences in the version below – how many can you spot?

68

PAIRING UP

Hedges – some like battlements, others demure and flowering – are often fundamental parts of gardens. Can you match up these hedge plant names?

Chinese Honeysuckle	*Ligustrum ovalifolium*
Holly	*Lonicera nitida*
Lavender	*Taxus baccata*
Privet	*Ilex aquifolium*
Yew	*Lavandula angustifolia*

———◇———

69

ENTICING BEES

Which herb was rubbed on the insides of skeps to encourage the presence of bees?

- Balm
- Fennel
- Mint
- Parsley
- Rosemary

70

HITCHING A LIFT!

Which flower, introduced into the Oxford Botanic Garden from Southern Italy in the 17th century, was spread along rail tracks by trains of the Great Western Railway (God's Wonderful Railway) during the late 1800s and later?

- *Cymbalaria muralis* (Oxford Weed or Ivy-leaved Toadflax)
- *Galium aparine* (Goosegrass)
- *Senecio squalidus* (Oxford Ragwort)

71

FRITILLARIA CONUNDRUM

Several fritillarias brighten our gardens, but which one is the Crown Imperial?

- *Fritillaria imperialis*
- *Fritillaria meleagris*
- *Fritillaria pallidiflora*

72

MEMORABLE VERSE

This popular verse by the Irish poet Thomas Moore
(1779–1852) is often quoted, but can you complete it?

'Tis the last rose of summer,
Left blooming alone;
All ...'

———◇———

73

VICAR'S SEED-SOWING ADVICE

In earlier years, seed-sowing guidance was often linked
with the church. Can you finish this saying?

'When the parson begins to read Genesis ...'

GARDENS IN LITERATURE

Who wrote the following, and can you complete it?

'God Almighty first planted a garden. And indeed it is ...'

———————◇———————

COTTAGE GARDEN REBUS

Spires of wide, funnel-shaped flowers. Can you name it?

 HOCK

76
SEED-SOWING PREDICTIONS

Can you finish this old seed-sowing rhyme?

'Sow pease (good Trull),
The moon is past full,
Fine seeds then sow,
Whilst ...'

———◇———

77
FLOWER REBUS

Masses of flowers popular with children.
Can you name it?

SNAP

78
FRENCHMAN'S DARLING

Which flower, given popularity by Joséphine de Beauharnais, wife of Napoléon Bonaparte, became known as Frenchman's Darling?

---◇---

79
STREWING FLOWERS FOR WEDDINGS

In earlier years, up to the 19th century, country bridal parties often walked to church on pathways strewn with plants. Which of these were a popular combination?

- Ash leaves
- Honeysuckle
- Rice
- Rushes
- Scattering of wheat
- Wild flowers

BENEFICIAL INSECT WORDSEARCH

Insects that eat garden pests are essential in a garden as they help to control pests without having to resort to the use of pesticides. Nineteen beneficial insects are hidden in this wordsearch – how many can you see?

- Anthocorid bug
- Braconid
- Brown lacewing
- Capsid bug
- Chalcid
- Damselfly
- Dragonfly
- Green lacewing
- Ground beetle
- Hoverfly
- Ichneumon fly
- Ladybird
- Mite
- Nabid bug
- Parasitic wasp
- Powdery lacewing
- Rove beetle
- Shield bug
- Stiletto fly

G	A	S	B	Y	L	F	O	T	T	E	L	I	T	S
R	N	H	C	I	A	Q	N	A	B	I	D	B	U	G
E	P	I	C	H	N	E	U	M	O	N	F	L	Y	N
E	E	E	W	H	Y	L	F	N	O	G	A	R	D	I
N	L	L	C	E	B	R	A	C	O	N	I	D	F	W
L	T	D	Y	D	C	A	P	S	I	D	B	U	G	E
A	E	B	B	C	H	A	L	C	I	D	X	F	H	C
C	E	U	F	V	E	Z	L	F	S	D	J	F	Y	A
E	B	G	Q	M	I	T	E	Y	S	X	D	L	L	L
W	E	Q	B	N	D	G	K	W	R	E	J	U	F	N
I	V	L	A	D	Y	B	I	R	D	E	H	P	R	W
N	O	N	Y	L	F	L	E	S	M	A	D	Z	E	O
G	R	O	U	N	D	B	E	E	T	L	E	W	V	R
P	S	A	W	C	I	T	I	S	A	R	A	P	O	B
A	N	T	H	O	C	O	R	I	D	B	U	G	H	P

81
KISSING RHYME

Gorse (*Ulex europaeus*) is claimed to indicate when kissing is permissible. Can you complete this rhyme?

'When gorse is out of bloom,
Kissing's ...'

---◇---

82
WHISKERS ON HORSES

Which shrub is said, when chewed by horses, to result in long whiskers on their lips?

- Common Gorse
- Dog Rose
- Pyracantha

83
FLOWERS IN LITERATURE

Who wrote the following, and can you continue it?

'I wandered lonely as a cloud,
That floats on high o'er vales and hills,
When all at once I saw ...'

---◇---

84
WEATHER FORECASTING

Can you finish this rhyme?

'If the oak's before the ash,
You will only get a splash,
But if ...'

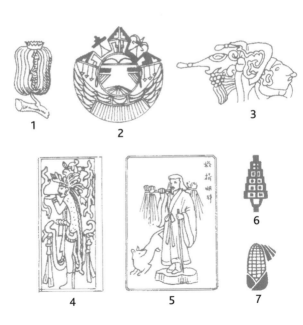

85

GODS, PATRONS,
BADGES AND SYMBOLS

Many plants, from tobacco to maize and rice, have been
given god-like status and become badges or used as
emblems of fertility. Here are a few – can you
identify them?

86
PROTECTING CARROTS

Carrot root-flies soon cause damage, but they can
be deterred without having to use chemical sprays.
Which of these three solutions will confuse them and
keep carrots safe?

• Strips of rags soaked in paraffin (kerosene) and placed
alongside the rows.
• Fresh lawn mowings placed alongside the rows.
• Garlic, leeks or onions planted around beds of carrots.

———◇———

87
FLOWERS IN LITERATURE

Who wrote the following, and can you complete it?

'And I will make thee beds of roses ...'

88

HERBACEOUS REBUS

Spikes of starry, white flowers in early summer.
Can you name it?

LILY

◇

89

FEMALE FERTILITY

In earlier centuries female fertility was especially
important and many women drank Tansy juice to ensure
they would bear children – but why Tansy?

90

EBBS AND FLOWS!

Some early weather forecasts relied on tidal ebbs and
flows. Can you complete the following early
English rhyme?

'If it raineth when it doth flow,
Then yoke your ox and go to plough,
But if it raineth ...'

91

HARVESTING TIME

Country rhymes that indicated the time to harvest crops
were just as popular as seed-sowing types. Can you
complete the following rhyme?

'If the moon shows a silver shield,
Be not afraid to reap your field,
But if ...'

92

HARVESTING APPLES

The time to harvest apples was often influenced by
country sayings. Can you complete the following rhyme?

'Till St Swithin's Day be past,
The apples ...'

———◇———

93

GRAFTING AND PRUNING
RHYME

The best time to graft and prune apple trees was said
to be when the moon's rays were increasing. Can you
complete this rhyme?

'From moon being changed,
Till past be the prime,
For grafting ...'

94

SLUG AND SNAIL REPELLENTS

These pernicious pests detest some plants, which can be used to give protection to neighbouring plants. Which of the following plants have this quality?

- *Hyssopus officinalis* (Hyssop)
- *Salvia officinalis* (Common Sage)
- *Salvia splendens* (Scarlet Sage)
- *Thymus spp.* (Thyme)

95

PLANT HERALDRY

Plants – and especially flowers – have long been used in heraldry. Try matching up these countries and flowers.

England	Thistle
Ireland	Leek
Scotland	Shamrock
Wales	Rose

SPOT THE DIFFERENCE

Growing culinary and medicinal herbs has been a part of
gardening for many hundreds of years.

Here is an illustration of a herb garden in the early 1500s.
There are ten differences between the original (opposite)
and the version below – how many can you spot?

97
FIERY FLOWER

Which of the following flowers was so prolific in its
native California that the Spaniards named the country
'The Land of Fire and Golden West'?

- *Eschscholzia californica*
- *Phlox drummondii*
- *Tagetes erecta*

98
LILY CONUNDRUM

Many lilies are grown in gardens. Can you sort out the
common and botanical names of these ones?

Lilium auratum	Leopard Lily
Lilium candidum	Tiger Lily
Lilium chalcedonicum	Golden-rayed Lily of Japan
Lilium pardalinum	Madonna Lily
Lilium tigrinum	Scarlet Turk's Cap Lily

99
GARDENING PROVERB

How does this proverb end?

'Let your prayers for a good crop be short – and ...'

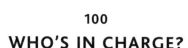

100
WHO'S IN CHARGE?

Which popular culinary herb when flourishing in a garden
is said to indicate that the mistress of the house rules?

- Aniseed
- Marjoram
- Parsley
- Rosemary
- Sage

101

LOVE APPLES

When first introduced into Britain, the fruits of which vegetable were thought to induce passion and wantonness?

- Cucumbers
- French Beans
- Radishes
- Tomatoes

———◇———

102

TOOTHACHE CURE

Parts of this plant could put dentists out of business! The cure was to soak pieces in hot honey and let the patient chew them slowly near the aching tooth. Which plant was it?

- Artichoke
- Clove
- Garlic
- Kidney Bean
- Radish

103

KENDAL GREEN

This was a popular colour during the Middle Ages
and resulted from a combination of two plants –
which are they?

- *Anthemis tinctoria* (Dyer's Chamomile)
- *Genista tinctoria* (Dyer's Greenweed)
- *Isatis tinctoria* (Dyer's Woad)
- *Morinda tinctoria* (Dyer's Mulberry)
- *Reseda luteola* (Dyer's Weld)

104

FIRE PROTECTION

Which plant is said to protect houses from lightning and
fire and, in some countries, was encouraged to grow on
thatched and tiled roofs?

- Daisy
- Heather
- Houseleek
- Moss
- Thyme

APPLE SPIDERMITE CROSSWORD

Apples are the most widely grown tree fruit and include dessert and culinary varieties (some are suitable for both uses). Here are twenty-three popular apple varieties; which ones can you fit into the spidermite on the opposite page? We have added eight key letters to help you.

- American Mother
- Beauty of Bath
- Blenheim Orange
- Bramley's Seedling
- Cox's Orange Pippin
- Delicious
- Discovery
- Egremont Russet
- Gala
- George Cave
- Granny Smith
- Grenadier
- James Grieve
- Jonagold
- Kidd's Orange Red
- Laxton's Superb
- Newton Wonder
- Orleans Reinette
- Ribston Pippin
- Spartan
- Sunset
- Tydeman's Late Orange
- Worcester Pearmain

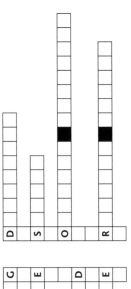

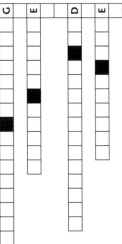

106
FORAGING NIBBLE

Widely seen on rubbish heaps and disturbed soil, this native plant has long been part of foraging diets. Among its common names are Bacon Weed, Lamb's Quarters, Pigweed and Wild Spinach, but what is its more usual countryside name?

- Borage
- Coriander
- Fat Hen
- Wild Cabbage
- Wild Garlic

107

PAIRING UP

Wisterias are some of the most spectacular flowering climbing plants. Here are three of them – can you match up the common and botanical names?

Wisteria floribunda	American Wisteria
Wisteria frutescens	Chinese Wisteria
Wisteria sinensis	Japanese Wisteria

◇

108

CACTUS REBUS

Popular cactus with long, prickly stems covered in funnel-shaped, magenta flowers. Can you name it?

CACTUS

EVENING AND NIGHT SCENTS

Many plants have deliciously scented flowers during the day, but which four of the following plants are especially known for their evening and night fragrances?

- *Hesperis matronalis*
- *Lobularia maritima*
- *Matthiola longipetala (M. bicornis)*
- *Mirabilis jalapa*
- *Oenothera biennis*
- *Primula florindae*

110

WATERLILY JUMBLEY

There are many waterlily varieties, but they mostly have the same genus name. What is it?

MAPHYNEA

111

GARDENING PROVERB

How does this proverb end?

'When God blesses the harvest there is enough for ...'

◇

112

FLOWERS IN LITERATURE

Here is a memorable Victorian poem. Can you complete
the first verse and name the poet?

'She wore a wreath of roses
The night that first we met ...'

113
TREE REBUS

Evergreen tree with inedible but attractive fruits.
Can you name it?

TREE

114
FORAGING JUMBLEY

This widespread native plant has a slender taproot that smells of garlic when crushed. Can you identify it?

CAJK-NI-TEH-HEEDG

115

FRUIT JUMBLEY

Raised in about 1850, this is perhaps the best-known dessert apple. Its name is hidden in the following letters.

XOC'S ANGERO NIPPIP

116

PLANTING RHYME

Planting rhymes have always been popular and here is one about the best time to plant potato tubers. Can you complete it?

'When you hear the cuckoo shout,
'Tis time ...'

117

ROSE PERFECTION

In 1799, Joséphine de Beauharnais, wife of Napoléon Bonaparte, bought *Chateau de Malmaison* and was inspirational in creating a magnificent rose garden. Where in France was the garden?

- Bordeaux
- Lyon
- Marseille
- Paris

118

PLAGUE ANTIDOTE

Which herb was part of the 'Vinegar of the Four Thieves', a French concoction which earlier enabled thieves in Marseille to enter plague houses with impunity?

- Garlic
- Rosemary
- Rue
- Tansy

119
SEED-SOWING PREDICTIONS

Can you finish this seed-sowing rhyme?

'When the elm leaf is as big as a mouse's ear,
Then to sow ...'

⬦

120
ARM BLISTERER

Which sprawling, wayside plant has been used by
vagrants to create blisters on arms to excite pity and to
encourage financial donations?

- *Anthriscus sylvestris* (Cow Parsley)
- *Calystegia sepium* (Hedge Bindweed)
- *Clematis vitalba* (Traveller's Joy)
- *Galium aparine* (Common Cleavers)
- *Galium mollugo* (Hedge Bedstraw)

PEAR VARIETY WORDSEARCH

Although slightly less popular than apples, there are many varieties of pears. How many of these fifteen varieties can you find in this wordsearch?

- Beth
- Beurre Hardy
- Beurre Superfin
- Concorde
- Conference
- Doyenne du Comice
- Durondeau
- Gorham
- Jargonelle
- Merton Pride
- Onward
- Packham's Triumph
- Seckle
- Thompson's
- Winter Nelis

P	A	M	F	Y	J	U	A	E	D	N	O	R	U	D
A	X	W	D	F	K	N	E	G	F	K	L	S	B	O
C	S	I	V	B	K	H	D	L	U	Y	T	X	E	Y
K	A	N	J	Z	J	A	R	G	O	N	E	L	L	E
H	X	T	H	O	M	P	S	O	N	S	N	B	R	N
A	B	E	U	R	R	E	S	U	P	E	R	F	I	N
M	C	R	Y	D	R	A	H	E	R	R	U	E	B	E
S	O	N	W	A	R	D	Q	K	C	K	J	L	T	D
T	Y	E	K	R	B	T	N	L	T	K	I	H	V	U
R	L	L	H	E	B	E	T	H	Q	H	L	I	T	C
I	Z	I	V	T	Q	D	V	P	K	Q	V	E	Y	O
U	L	S	C	E	D	I	R	P	N	O	T	R	E	M
M	A	H	R	O	G	K	H	G	T	H	T	N	V	I
P	A	I	H	T	E	C	N	E	R	E	F	N	O	C
H	S	I	B	H	Q	Q	C	O	N	C	O	R	D	E

122
WHIN, GORSE OR FURZE?

Gorse (*Ulex europaeus*) has several common names, but which parts of the British Isles most usually use Whin, Gorse or Furze? Can you match up these names and areas?

Furze	In the north
Gorse	In the east
Whin	In the south

———◇———

123
DYING OF LAUGHTER

Which highly prized bulb has dried stigmas used as a disinfectant, dye, condiment and a medicine? They are also said to cause uncontrollable laughter.

- Daffodil
- Lily
- Saffron Crocus
- Tulip

124

CAT'S DELIGHT

Nepeta or Kattesminthe (*Nepeta cataria* and now known as Catnip or Catnep) was grown in English gardens as early as 1263. It attracts cats but, strangely, they are more likely to destroy transplanted plants than those raised from seed and not replanted. This has encouraged the following saying – can you complete it?

'If you set [plant] it, the cats will get it,
If you ...'

---◇---

125

FLOWERS IN SONGS

Who wrote the following, and can you finish the line?

'Tiptoe through the ...'

126

MAGICAL SHRUB

The North American tree *Hamamelis virginiana* gained its name Witch Hazel from the way early settlers used it – but how?

---◇---

127

DETERRING MOLES

Moles disturb soil with their tunnels and mounds, but they can be deterred without causing them harm. Which border plant has a mole-repelling quality if planted near the runs?

- *Corydalis lutea* (Yellow Fumitory)
- *Dicentra spectabilis* (Bleeding Heart)
- *Euphorbia lathyrus* (Caper Spurge)
- *Helleborus orientalis* (Lenten Rose)
- *Pulmonaria officinalis* (Jerusalem Cowslip)

128
FOOLING GREENFLY

Nasturtiums especially attract greenfly (aphids), but they can be protected by putting a plant nearby that attracts hoverflies that feed on greenfly. Which plant is it?

- *Bellis perennis* (Double Daisy)
- *Cosmos bipinnatus* (Cosmea)
- *Dianthus barbatus* (Sweet William)
- *Hibiscus trionum* (Flower-of-an-hour)
- *Tagetes patula* (French Marigold)

129
SUNDIAL INSCRIPTION

These are many and varied, but can you complete the following popular inscription?

'Time wastes our bodies and our wits,
But we …'

130

ENDURING THYME

Few pieces of literature are so well known as:

'I know a bank whereon the wild thyme blows'.

Can you continue the quotation?

---◇---

131

JAILHOUSE BLUES!

Up to the beginning of the 19th century, a bunch containing two popular herbs would be placed at the side of a prisoner in the dock to protect court officials from catching 'jail fever'. Which two herbs were they?

- Hyssop
- Rue
- Southernwood
- Thyme
- Winter Savory

STRONGLY SCENTED

The late 17th-century English garden designer and writer
John Evelyn claimed that this aromatic shrub could be
detected thirty leagues (about 78 miles) off the coast of
Spain – what a claim! Which shrub was he talking about?

- Common Sage
- Lavender
- Rosemary

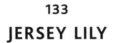

JERSEY LILY

Which popular bulbous flower has the same common
name as Lillie (Lily) Langtry, who was a mistress of
Edward VII, future King of England, while he was
Prince of Wales?

- *Amaryllis belladonna*
- *Hyacinthus orientalis*
- *Muscari armeniacum*

134

SHRIEKING PLANT

Which plant was said to grow under the gallows of murderers and to utter shrieks that caused death when pulled from the ground?

- *Aegopodium podagraria* (Ground Elder)
- *Conium maculatum* (Hemlock)
- *Hyoscyamus niger* (Henbane)
- *Mandragora officinarum* (Mandrake)

135

FRENCH CONNECTION

The French knew the value of this plant and used it in wardrobes and drawers to keep clothes free from moths and other insects. It became known as Garde Robe, but which plant is it?

- *Artemisia abrotanum* (Southernwood)
- *Moluccella laevis* (Bells of Ireland)
- *Monarda didyma* (Bergamot)
- *Ruta graveolens* (Rue)

WART FOLKLORE

Removing warts through folklore has been a thriving industry. One method was for the patient to visit an ash tree, with each wart then pricked by a new pin later pushed into the tree's bark. This needed to be accompanied by a chant – can you complete it?

'Ashen tree, Ashen tree,
Pray ...'

TEASING PLANT

What is the common name of the plant with recurved bracts on its flowerheads that earlier were used to raise the nap on cloth?

- Butterbur
- Cotton Thistle
- Devil's Bit
- Field Scabious
- Fuller's Teasel

138

FASHIONS IN FLOWERS

Passion for specific flowers has varied throughout the ages, with some being in fashion and others not. Here are a few of the many flowers that have been especially popular – can you name their countries and the times at which they were capturing most attention?

1. Lotus
2. Violet
3. Rose
4. Wallflower and Rosemary
5. Lily
6. *Mirabilis jalapa* (Marvel of Peru)
7. Fritillary
8. Tulip
9. Hyacinth
10. Auricula
11. *Bellis perennis* (Double Daisy)
12. Ranunculus
13. Carnation
14. Forget-me-not
15. Dahlia
16. Fuchsia
17. Camellia
18. Mignonette
19. White Lilac
20. Pansy

139

PAIRING UP

How many of these butterfly-attracting plants can you match up?

Blue Beard	*Dianthus barbatus*
Butterfly Bush	*Caryopteris × clandonensis*
Ice Plant	*Buddleja davidii*
Michaelmas Daisy	*Sedum spectabile*
Sweet William	*Aster novi-belgii*

140

LOVING SIGNALS

Legends from South Sea Islands suggest that flowers from this plant offer amorous messages: a flower worn behind the left ear indicates 'I desire a lover'; behind the right ear 'I have a lover'; and behind both ears 'I have one lover, but desire another'. Which flower is it?

- Red Hibiscus
- Red Petunia
- Rose-pink Love-in-a-Mist

141

DRUNKEN BLISS!

Slugs and snails can be lured into glass jars sunk to their rims near plants and half-filled with an elixir they cannot resist. What is it?

- Paraffin and water
- Salt and water
- Soap and water
- Sugar and beer

142

PAIRING UP

There are many bamboos that grow in temperate climates and some have unusually shaped or coloured canes. Can you match these up?

Black-stemmed Bamboo	*Chimonobambusa quadrangularis*
Golden Bamboo	*Phyllostachys nigra*
Square-stemmed Bamboo	*Phyllostachys aurea*

PROTECTING ROSES

Roses are soon damaged by greenfly, but these can be
deterred by growing a culinary herb close by.
Which one is it?

- Chives
- Mint
- Parsley
- Sage
- Thyme

PAIRING UP

How many of these garden weeds can you match up?

Chickweed	*Convolvulus arvensis*
Dandelion	*Urtica dioica*
Field Bindweed	*Galium odoratum*
Ground Elder	*Taraxacum officinale*
Stinging Nettle	*Aegopodium podagraria*
Woodruff	*Stellaria media*

SPIDERMITE CROSSWORD HOUSEPLANT

Most homes have several houseplants, perhaps grouped on windowsills, on tables or, if large, on the floor.

Here are thirty popular houseplants primarily grown for their attractive leaves. Which ones can you fit into the spidermite crossword on the opposite page? We have added eight key letters to help you.

• Abutilon	• Grevillea
• Anthurium	• Hedera
• Aspidistra	• Iresine
• Begonia	• Maranta
• Caladium	• Monstera
• Chlorophytum	• Philodendron
• Coleus	• Pilea
• Cordyline	• Sansevieria
• Croton	• Saxifraga
• Dieffenbachia	• Scindapsus
• Dizygotheca	• Stromanthe
• Dracaena	• Syngonium
• Fatsia	• Tolmiea
• Ficus	• Tradescantia
• Fittonia	• Yucca

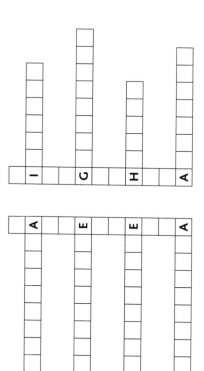

146

PAIRING UP

A fly's heaven is sure to include several of these 'stinkers'
of the plant world. Can you match up these smells with
the plants?

Aristolochia macrophylla	Carrion and garlic
Fritillaria imperialis	Animal
Lysichiton americanus	Manure
Lysichiton camtschatcensis	Putrid
Trillium erectum	Foxy

147

BULB JUMBLEY

Widely known as Glory of the Snow, which genus of
bulbs is hidden in these letters?

DOONAXIOCH

KEEPING BEES AT BAY

The Romans cultivated this vegetable both to eat and keep bees at bay. They mashed the soft tips of shoots in oil and rubbed it over their skin. Which vegetable was this?

- Asparagus
- Calabrese
- Chives
- Garlic
- Onion

BEAUTIFUL ITALIAN LADIES

Which highly poisonous wild plant, shrubby and with dingy purple, bell-like flowers and smooth black berries, was used by Italian ladies to give extra brilliance to their eyes?

- Deadly Nightshade
- Foxglove
- Henbane
- Mullein

150
VERSATILE NATIVE PLANT

Few plants are as obliging as this widespread plant, seen in meadows and pastures, lawns, waste ground and alongside roads. Apart from having young leaves and flower buds for adding to salads, the roots can be roasted to produce a 'coffee' which is almost undistinguishable from real coffee and has the bonus of not containing caffeine. Which is it?

- Borage
- Curled Dock
- Dandelion
- Horseradish
- Tansy

———————◇———————

151
VEGETABLE RHYME

Can you complete the following amusing rhyme?

'I always eat peas with honey,
I've done it all my life,
They ...'

152

PAIRING UP

Several members of the *Philodendron* genus are ideal houseplants. Can you rearrange these philodendrons to give the correct common and botanical names?

Philodendron bipennifolium	Sweetheart Plant
Philodendron bipinnatifidum	Fiddle-leaf Philodendron
Philodendron domesticum	Tree Philodendron
Philodendron erubescens	Elephant's Ear Philodendron
Philodendron scandens	Blushing Philodendron

153

PUBLICISING CUCUMBERS!

Samuel Johnson (1709–1784), in his *Tour of the Hebrides*, clearly was not enthused by cucumbers. Can you complete his words?

'A cucumber should be well sliced, and dressed with pepper and vinegar, and then ...'

154

APOTHECARY'S ROSE

This legendary rose, known since before the 14th century, has red, semi-double flowers with petals that have the ability to preserve their scent when dried. What is its name?

- *Rose alba* 'Celestial'
- *Rosa alba* 'Maxima'
- *Rosa centifolia*
- *Rosa gallica* 'Belle de Crécy'
- *Rosa gallica* 'Officinalis'

155

DUTCH DUO

With popular names such as Woodbine and Honeysuckle, there are two well-known forms of *Lonicera periclymenum*. Can you provide the botanical names of the following?

- The Early Dutch Honeysuckle
- The Late Dutch Honeysuckle

VIOLET-SCENTED ROOTS

Iris 'Florentina' (earlier known as *Iris germanica florentina*) has been used in toilet preparations for 2,000 years. It has also been known as White Flower de Luce and Flower de Luce of Florence. What is it more usually called?

- Angelica
- Burdock
- Liquorice
- Orris Root
- Valerian

OPIUM POPPY

There are many species of poppy grown in our gardens, but which one is notorious for its narcotic properties?

- *Papaver nudicaule*
- *Papaver orientale*
- *Papaver rhoeas*
- *Papaver somniferum*

158

WEATHER RHYME

The countryside was steeped in weather wisdom.
Can you complete the following?

'If the cock moults before the hen,
We shall have weather thick and thin;
But if ...'

———⬦———

159

PAIRING UP

Several plants have particular times of the year in their
common names. Can you match these plants?

Christmas Rose	*Chimonanthus praecox*
Easter Lily	*Aster novi-belgii*
Michaelmas Daisy	*Helleborus niger*
Winter Jasmine	*Lilium longiflorum*
Winter Sweet	*Jasminum nudiflorum*

PAIRING UP

Ivies are popular and reliable climbing plants for covering walls and trellises. Can you rearrange these ivies to give the correct botanical and common names?

Hedera canariensis	Irish Ivy
Hedera colchica	Common Ivy
Hedera helix	Persian Ivy
Hedera hibernica	Canary Island Ivy

PAIRING UP

Scented garden shrubs that flower in winter are highly prized. Can you rearrange the botanical and common names of these shrubs?

Chimonanthus praecox	Mezereon
Daphne mezereum	Winter Sweet
Hamamelis japonica	Chinese Witch Hazel
Hamamelis mollis	Ozark Witch Hazel
Hamamelis vernalis	Japanese Witch Hazel

STRAWBERRY VARIETY WORDSEARCH

These are the most popular soft fruit and each year millions are eaten in combination with cream and a dusting of sugar. How many of these nineteen varieties can you spot in this wordsearch?

- Alexandria
- Aromel
- Baron Solemacher
- Cambridge Vigour
- Domanil
- Elvira
- Gento
- Grandee
- Harvester
- Ostara
- Pandora
- Pantagruella
- Redgauntlet
- Royal Sovereign
- Selva
- Tantallon
- Tenira
- Totem
- Troubador

B	A	R	O	N	S	O	L	E	M	A	C	H	E	R
S	L	O	F	N	O	L	L	A	T	N	A	T	E	E
Z	E	Y	A	S	X	L	H	W	O	H	M	O	D	D
S	X	A	P	Z	A	S	A	L	S	X	B	T	N	G
P	A	L	L	F	L	H	R	E	T	H	R	E	A	A
W	N	S	H	S	L	P	V	M	A	X	I	M	R	U
F	D	O	G	R	E	X	E	O	R	H	D	W	G	N
W	R	V	E	O	U	S	S	R	A	P	G	Z	J	T
P	I	E	N	D	R	A	T	A	S	L	E	L	S	L
X	A	R	T	A	G	R	E	R	A	W	V	F	D	E
A	P	E	O	B	A	I	R	O	A	R	I	N	E	T
V	W	I	H	U	T	V	Z	D	L	H	G	K	L	Z
L	A	G	P	O	N	L	I	N	A	M	O	D	S	D
E	J	N	L	R	A	E	S	A	W	L	U	F	S	H
S	P	F	S	T	P	H	Z	P	S	C	R	D	J	F

PAIRING UP

Several members of the fig family are ideal houseplants.
Can you rearrange these figs to give the correct common
and botanical names?

Ficus benghalensis	Bo Tree
Ficus benjamina	Rubber Plant
Ficus deltoidea	Creeping Fig
Ficus elastica	Bengal Fig
Ficus pumila	Weeping Fig
Ficus religiosa	Mistletoe Fig

———◇———

164

ADDING SPICINESS

Flowers were earlier added to ales and wines to create a
more spicy flavour. Which one was called Sops-in-Wine?

- Clove Gilloflower
- Heartsease
- Soapwort
- Wallflower

165

YUCCAS IN PRINT

Fibres of the Joshua Tree (*Yucca brevifolia*), native to southwest North America, were earlier used to create paper for printing newspapers. Which British newspaper was printed on it?

- *The Daily Telegraph*
- *Methodist Recorder*
- *The Scotsman*
- *The Field*

---◇---

166

PIPE DREAM

The knotted roots of this shrub, known in France as *La Bruyère*, were earlier used to make Briar Pipes. What is its botanical name?

- *Buxus sempervirens*
- *Erica arborea*
- *Erica carnea*
- *Ruscus aculeatus*

PAIRING UP

Shrubs with aromatic leaves often have a cooling influence
on the air around them. Can you arrange the common
and botanical names of these shrubs?

Aloysia citrodora	Mexican Orange Blossom
Calycanthus floridus	Rosemary
Choisya ternata	Carolina Allspice
Cistus ladanifer	Lemon Verbena
Rosmarinus officinalis	Gum Cistus

———————◇———————

VEGETABLE REBUS

These are one of the staple vegetables of the Western
world and botanically known as *Solanum tuberosum*. Can
you name them?

A

169

VEGETABLE JUMBLEY

Sometimes known as Black Salsify, it has sweetly flavoured fleshy roots with black skin and white flesh. Can you decipher it from these letters?

ZONERRASCO

170

A BOUNTY ON THIS FOOD!

Which Pacific Island fruit was associated with Captain Bligh and the mutiny on the *Bounty* in 1789?

- Avocado Pear
- Breadfruit
- Jack Fruit (Jak Fruit)
- Papaya

EARLY DIGGING AND PLOUGHING TOOLS

During the 17th century, tools for digging, trenching and ditching were becoming increasingly popular, although many had been known in some form since Biblical times. This is an illustration of land-improving and cultivating tools from Blith's *The English Improver Improved*, of 1652. How many can you name?

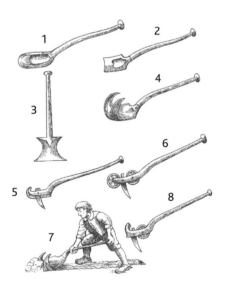

172

PAIRING UP

There are several species of jasmine grown in our gardens. Can you rearrange the following to give the correct common and botanical names?

Jasminum humile	Winter-flowering Jasmine
Jasminum mesnyi	Pink Jasmine
Jasminum nudiflorum	Common White Jasmine
Jasminum officinale	Primrose Jasmine
Jasminum polyanthum	Italian Yellow Jasmine

———◇———

173

FRUIT JUMBLEY

This is the most popular variety of grape grown in greenhouses. Can you decipher it from these letters?

CLABK BURGHHAM

BRIDESMAID'S DELIGHT

Several species of *Achillea* are grown in flower borders
in our gardens, but which one had the evocative name
'Seven Years' Love' and was carried by bridesmaids
at country weddings?

- *Achillea clavennae*
- *Achillea filipendulina*
- *Achillea millefolium*
- *Achillea ptarmica*
- *Achillea tomentosa*

PAIRING UP

Mints are steeped in common names, but can you match
up these popular ones with their botanical names?

Mentha × gracilis	Pineapple Mint
Mentha × piperita	Applemint
Mentha spicata	Peppermint
Mentha suaveolens	Spearmint
Mentha suaveolens	'Variegata' Ginger Mint

BUTCHER'S BROOM

The stiff, prickly branches of this evergreen garden shrub
have stiff, scratchy, modified leaves which were used
by butchers to scour their working blocks. What is its
botanical name?

- *Berberis vulgaris*
- *Ilex aquifolium*
- *Pyracantha*
- *Ruscus aculeatus*
- *Ulex europaeus*

SHRUB REBUS

You will easily recognise this late winter- and spring
flowering evergreen shrub. If you can't, don't get the
hump over it!

LIA

AMERICAN SUNDIAL INSCRIPTION

These are usually brief and apt. Can you complete the following common inscription?

'Hours fly,
Flowers die
New days,
New ...'

---◇---

PAIRING UP

Several plants have scented roots. Can you match up these plants and their scents?

Acorus calamus	Rose
Geum rivale	Liquorice
Glycyrrhiza glabra	Violets
Iris florentina	Camphor
Rhodiola rosea	Beer

180

FRUIT JUMBLEY

This succulent tropical fruit is best known for its fruits which contain a large number of seeds. Its name is hidden in the following letters.

GRANPOMEATE

181

PAIRING UP

No garden is free from 'weeds'; some are pernicious and without fail appear each year. Can you match up these weeds with their botanical names?

Common Horsetail	*Ranunculus ficaria*
Couch Grass	*Equisetum arvense*
Field Bindweed	*Agropyron repens*
Ground Elder	*Convolvulus arvensis*
Lesser Celandine	*Aegopodium podagraria*

VEGETABLE WORDSEARCH

Growing vegetables is becoming increasingly popular.
How many of these twenty-three vegetables can you spot
in this wordsearch?

- Asparagus
- Beetroot
- Broad beans
- Broccoli
- Brussels sprouts
- Cabbage
- Calabrese
- Carrots
- Cauliflower
- Celery
- Courgettes
- French beans

- Globe artichokes
- Leeks
- Lettuce
- Marrow
- Onions
- Parsnips
- Peas
- Runner beans
- Sweetcorn
- Tomatoes
- Turnips

B	X	H	C	R	N	M	C	A	B	B	A	G	E	L
F	R	E	N	C	H	B	E	A	N	S	X	V	X	E
S	U	U	Q	X	K	S	L	S	V	N	K	L	A	E
S	N	E	S	S	W	E	E	T	C	O	R	N	S	K
T	N	C	K	S	D	K	R	L	X	I	X	K	P	S
O	E	U	L	V	E	W	Y	D	Q	N	J	W	A	B
R	R	T	C	A	U	L	I	F	L	O	W	E	R	R
R	B	T	Q	P	A	R	S	N	I	P	S	L	A	O
A	E	E	X	S	W	K	V	S	J	L	E	Q	G	A
C	A	L	A	B	R	E	S	E	P	D	J	A	U	D
V	N	W	S	I	L	O	C	C	O	R	B	J	S	B
Q	S	X	S	E	T	T	E	G	R	U	O	C	W	E
T	O	M	A	T	O	E	S	P	I	N	R	U	T	A
W	O	R	R	A	M	B	E	E	T	R	O	O	T	N
G	L	O	B	E	A	R	T	I	C	H	O	K	E	S

183

PAIRING UP

Several species of small bulbous plants are often confused.
Can you match the common names to these bulbs?

Chionodoxa	Snowflake
Galanthus	Glory of the Snow
Leucojum	Snowdrop

---◇---

184

VEGETABLE JUMBLEY

Used in winter and spring salads, the hearts are white,
crisp and slightly bitter. What is hidden here?

CYCHOIR

185
IRISH MOSS JUMBLEY

An extract from this seaweed, popularly known as Irish Moss, has been used in table jellies, blancmanges, ice creams, salad dressings and soups as an emulsifier. Its name is hidden in the following letters.

RAGACREEN

186
PERIWINKLE APHRODISIAC

Which well-known early herbalist said: 'The leaves of the lesser periwinkle, if eaten by man and wife together, will cause love between them'?

- Nicholas Culpeper (1616–1654)
- Leonhart Fuchs (1501–1566)
- John Gerard (1545–1612)
- William Turner (1508–1568)

BENEFICIAL GARDEN CREATURES WORDSEARCH

There are several garden creatures that eat insect pests. Seven of them are hidden in this wordsearch – how many can you see?

S	H	Z	G	U	S	J	T	S	V
L	E	J	U	S	E	O	Q	E	K
O	D	D	V	P	A	S	V	P	J
W	G	Q	E	D	K	G	S	G	V
W	E	V	S	P	I	D	E	R	S
O	H	S	G	H	I	G	K	U	Z
R	O	F	O	Z	R	T	U	G	K
M	G	V	R	G	U	E	N	S	V
S	S	K	F	K	S	U	W	E	U
G	Z	G	V	Z	V	G	Q	S	C

- Centipedes
- Frogs
- Hedgehogs
- Shrews
- Slow-worms
- Spiders
- Toads

BRIGHTENING WAYSIDE HEDGES

Clematis vitalba clambers over hedges, and from late summer into winter bears fluffy flowerheads. It has several names – two are found below. Which are they?

- Mountain Clematis
- Old Man's Beard
- Traveller's Joy
- Woodbine

◇

FRUIT REBUS

This succulent fruit is related to plums and gages.
What is it?

ACE

190
VEGETABLE JUMBLEY

This now rarely grown leafy vegetable has a royal connection. Can you name the plant?

GODO GINK RENHY

191
COASTAL FOOD JUMBLEY

This is a seaweed earlier used in South Wales, Ireland and some other European countries as a breakfast food. Can you unscramble it?

RAVEL

192
BEAUX BEWARE!

Predicting future husbands was part of country life and especially employed by young maidens. Can you complete this rhyme?

'Ivy, Ivy, I love you,
In my bosom I put you,
The first ...'

193
COCKROACH DETERRENT

These pernicious insects are nature's survivors and are claimed to eat anything except putty and cucumber. However, a native wild plant is also said to drive them away – which one?

- *Conium maculatum* (Hemlock)
- *Echium vulgare* (Viper's Bugloss)
- *Lamium album* (White Dead Nettle)
- *Papaver rhoeas* (Common Poppy)
- *Verbascum blattaria* (Moth Mullein)

FLOWERING HOUSEPLANT WORDSEARCH

Flowering houseplants are popular. How many of the following can you spot in this wordsearch?

- Acalypha
- Anthurium
- Aphelandra
- Begonia
- Beloperone
- Bougainvillea
- Bouvardia
- Clianthus
- Columnea
- Cuphea
- Episcia
- Gardenia
- Hoya
- Kalanchoe
- Pachystachys
- Passiflora
- Plumbago
- Saintpaulia
- Spathiphyllum
- Stephanotis
- Streptocarpus

P	A	C	H	Y	S	T	A	C	H	Y	S	J	S	E
S	N	E	P	L	G	J	K	C	S	O	L	X	I	O
K	T	M	L	A	C	A	A	Z	A	K	Y	B	T	H
B	H	R	U	L	S	L	R	I	L	L	T	A	O	C
B	U	A	E	L	I	S	I	D	C	A	Y	Z	N	N
E	R	R	Z	P	L	V	I	A	E	S	K	P	A	A
N	I	D	B	C	T	Y	N	F	N	N	I	A	H	L
O	U	N	K	B	O	O	H	I	L	T	I	P	P	A
R	M	A	S	X	S	L	C	P	A	O	H	A	E	K
E	A	L	S	K	Z	T	U	A	I	G	R	U	T	Z
P	B	E	G	O	N	I	A	M	R	H	U	A	S	A
O	S	H	C	U	P	H	E	A	N	P	T	O	A	L
L	L	P	L	U	M	B	A	G	O	E	U	A	B	J
E	T	A	I	L	U	A	P	T	N	I	A	S	P	B
B	O	U	V	A	R	D	I	A	X	J	Z	L	J	S

195

BIRD OMENS

During Saxon times the following rhyme was chanted to protect some birds. Can you complete it?

'The robin and the red-breast,
The martin and the swallow,
If ye ...'

196

CHURCH TITHES

Earlier, paying tithes to the local church often caused irritation to villagers. Can you complete this Saxon rhyme?

'We've cheated the Parson, we'll cheat him again,
Why should the vicar have one in ten?
One in ..'

197
PROTECTING SEEDS

Mice are often attracted to newly sown seeds, but can be deterred by putting pieces of this shrub's prickly stems half-buried along the rows. Can you name the shrub?

- Butcher's Broom
- Firethorn
- Gorse
- Holly

———◇———

198
FOOT-ROT CURE!

Country people working on the land often lined the insides of their boots with fresh leaves to soothe aching and burning feet. Which tree bears these leaves?

- Alder
- Aspen
- Beech
- Goat Willow
- Sweet Chestnut

VERSATILE CULINARY HERB

This herb has dried seeds used to flavour cakes, bread, rolls, cheese dishes, salads, pork, lamb and sausages. Which is it?

- Aniseed
- Caraway
- Coriander
- Dill
- Fennel

ANSWERS

1: PAIRING UP
- *Anethum graveolens* (Dill)
- *Anthriscus cerefolium* (Chervil)
- *Carum carvi* (Caraway)
- *Glycyrrhiza glabra* (Liquorice)
- *Melissa officinalis* (Balm / Bee Balm / Lemon Balm)
- *Monarda didyma* (Bergamot / Oswego Tea)

2: ROSE JUMBLEY
- Jacques Cartier (a Portland-type rose)

3: FLOWERS IN LITERATURE
- *Romeo and Juliet* – William Shakespeare (1564–1616)

4: SHRUB REBUS
- *Hippophae rhamnoides*

5: COMMON NAME CONUNDRUM
- *Viola tricolor*

6: BAD LUCK AND GOOD LUCK PLANTS
1. Artemisia – good luck
2. Cherry blossom – bad luck
3. Cherry tree – good luck
4. Four-leaved clover – good luck
5. Elder – good luck
6. Hawthorn (indoors) – bad luck
7. Hawthorn (outdoors) – good luck
8. Lavender – good luck
9. Rosemary – good luck
10. White heather – good luck

7: UNUSUAL FRAGRANCE
- *Heliotropium arborescens*

8: THE CRYSTAL PALACE
• *Punch*

9: CULINARY HERB WORDSEARCH

A	T	H	Y	M	E	X	P	L	V	C	S	D	S	A
N	N	A	S	C	C	Z	O	I	D	K	L	G	N	V
I	I	W	N	E	G	A	S	V	J	H	F	G	L	B
S	M	E	G	S	V	V	S	R	U	E	E	A	I	H
E	R	T	R	B	Y	L	Y	E	G	L	N	R	Q	S
E	E	F	G	H	J	B	H	H	I	O	N	L	U	I
D	D	Y	A	W	A	R	A	C	F	V	E	I	O	D
Y	N	L	Y	E	L	S	A	A	P	A	L	C	R	A
R	A	H	J	Q	S	E	T	B	G	J	N	I	R	R
E	I	R	S	D	K	G	E	C	S	E	G	H	C	E
G	R	R	A	L	A	G	L	L	V	O	R	P	E	S
N	O	O	I	R	V	B	N	M	N	Z	C	B	D	R
I	C	S	O	R	O	S	E	M	A	R	Y	E	I	O
G	A	B	A	Y	M	A	R	J	O	R	A	M	L	H
B	A	L	M	B	E	R	G	A	M	O	T	S	L	A

10: EMPRESS JOSÉPHINE
• Mignonette

11: WEATHER-FORECASTING FLOWER
• *Anagallis arvensis*

12: BOTANIC GARDENS
• Cambridge Botanic Garden – 1831
• Chelsea Physic Garden – 1673
• Oxford Botanic Garden – 1621

13: WALL SHRUB JUMBLEY
• Pyracantha

14: ANNUAL FLOWER JUMBLEY
• Poached Egg Flower

15: TULIP MANIA
- 1634 to 1637

16: EARLY GRAFTING
1. Saw
2. Large knife, with a chisel head
3. Pruning knife
4. Chisel with a wimble bit (for boring a hole)
5. Mallet
6. Vine knife
7. Slicing knife for fine cuts
8. Grafting chisel
9. Hammer with a file and pearcer (piercer)
10. Grafting knife, with a ring or button to enable it to hang from a girdle

17: FLOWER SONG
- Edelweiss

18: CONIFER JUMBLEY
- Cedar of Lebanon

19: HERB JUMBLEY
- Alecost

20: CHAUCER'S TIME CLOCK
- Daisy

21: SPOT THE DIFFERENCE

22: PAIN-EASING HERBS
Non-pain-easing herbs:
- Herb Christopher
- Monkey Flower

23: GRAVES OF INNOCENT PEOPL E
- White Lily

24: FLOWER-SELLER CRIES
'Who'll buy my lavender, fresh lavender,
Sweet blooming lavender, who'll buy?'

25: TEA ROSE LEGACY
The land used by the earlier plant nursery is now the campus for Brunel University. Incidentally, the rose 'Lady Hillingdon' is still available from specialist rose nurseries.

26: INEBRIATE SOLUTION
- White Heather

27: WITCHCRAFT PROTECTION
- Rosemary

28: PAIRING UP
- *Araucaria araucana* – Monkey Puzzle
- *Calocedrus decurrens* – Incense Cedar
- *Cedrus atlantica* – Atlas Cedar
- *Cupressus sempervirens* – Italian Cypress
- *Ginkgo biloba* – Maidenhair Tree
- *Taxus baccata* – English Yew

29: APPLE JUMBLEY
- Bramley's Seedling

30: TEA ROSE REDOLENCE
- Freshly opened packet of tea (but not tarry Lapsang)

31: AGEING SUPERSTITION
- Acorn

32: WOUND-HEALING HERBS
Non-healing herbs:
- Dandelion
- Hedge Garlic

33: VEGETABLE ACCIDENTS
- Broad beans

34: GARDEN PEST SPIDERMITE CROSSWORD

35: GOOD LUCK VEGETABLE
- Chicory

36: RHEUMATISM PROTECTION
- Nutmeg

37: PLUM JUMBLEY
- Victoria

38: CHERRY JUMBLEY
- Napoleon Bigarreau

39: PAIRING UP
- *Aponogeton distachyos*
- *Butomus umbellatus*
- *Calla palustris*
- *Eichhornia crassipes*
- *Hottonia palustris*
- *Orontium aquaticum*

40: PEAR JUMBLEY
- Conference

41: PAIRING UP
- Blushing Bromeliad *Neoregelia carolinae*
- Coral Berry – *Aechmea fulgens*
- Pheasant Leaf *Cryptanthus fosterianus*
- Queen's Tears *Billbergia nutans*
- Red Pineapple *Ananas bracteatus*
- Zebra Plant – *Cryptanthus zonatus*

42: GARDENING QUOTATION
'The best place to seek God is in a garden. You can dig for him there.'
George Bernard Shaw (1856–1950)

43: PAIRING UP
- Devil's Backbone – *Kalanchoe daigremontiana*
- Panda Bear – *Kalanchoe tomentosa*
- Partridge-breasted Aloe – *Aloe variegata*
- Pearl Plant – *Haworthia margaritifera*
- Pig's Ears – *Cotyledon orbiculata*
- Tiger Jaws – *Faucaria tigrina*

44: GARDENING QUOTATION
'God made rainy days so that gardeners could get the housework done.'
Anonymous

45: KNOW YOUR ONIONS!
1. *Allium cepa* – Onion
2. *Asparagus officinalis* – Asparagus

3. *Beta vulgaris* – Beetroot
4. *Brassica oleracea* – Cabbages
(wide range, from cabbages to Brussels Sprouts and Cauliflower)
5. *Capsicum annuum* – Sweet Pepper
6. *Capsicum frutescens* – Tabasco Pepper and Hot Peppers
7. *Cichorium endiva* – Endive
8. *Cichorium intybus* – Chicory
9. *Daucus carota* – Carrot
10. *Lactuca sativa* – Lettuce
11. *Lotus tetragonolobus* – Asparagus Pea
12. *Lycopersicon esculentum* – Tomato
13. *Phaseolus coccineus* – Scarlet Runner
14. *Phaseolus vulgaris* – French and Runner Beans
15. *Pisum sativum* – Garden Pea
16. *Raphanus sativus* – Radish
17. *Solanum melongena* – Aubergine
18. *Solanum tuberosum* – Potato
19. *Vicia faba* – Broad Bean
20. *Zea mays* – Sweetcorn (Maize)

46: PAIRING UP
- Bird's Nest Fern – *Asplenium nidus*
- Button Fern – *Pellaea rotundifolia*
- Hen-and-Chickens Fern – *Asplenium bulbiferum*
- Maidenhair Fern – *Adiantum raddianum*
- Staghorn Fern – *Platycerium bifurcatum*
- Table Fern – *Pteris cretica*

47: CROP VALUE FORECASTS
'If it freezes on St Thomas's Day,
The price of corn will fall,
If it be mild, the price will rise.'
(St Thomas's Day is 21 December)

48: FRUIT JUMBLEY
- Boysenberry

49: ROYAL ASSOCIATION
- Good King Henry

51: VALENTINE'S DAY RHYME

'The rose is red, the violet's blue,
Pinks are sweet and so are you.'

52: WEATHER RHYME

'When the cuckoo comes to the bare thorn,
Sell your cow and buy your corn;
But when she comes to the full bit,
Sell your corn and your sheep.'

53: PAIRING UP

- Bishop's Cap Cactus – *Astrophytum myriostigma*
- Bunny's Ears – *Opuntia microdasys*
- Old Man Cactus – *Cephalocereus senilis*
- Peanut Cactus – *Chamaecereus silvestrii*
- Rat's Tail Cactus – *Aporocactus flagelliformis*
- Silver Torch Cactus – *Cleistocactus strausii*

54: GARDENING QUOTATION
'How fair is a garden amid the trials and passions of existence.'
Benjamin Disraeli (1804–1881)

55: PAIRING UP
- Bamboo Palm – *Rhapis excelsa*
- Belmore Sentry Palm – *Howea belmoreana*
- Dwarf Fan Palm – *Chamaerops humilis*
- Fishtail Palm – *Caryota mitis*
- Kentia Palm – *Howea forsteriana*

56: GARDENING QUOTATION
'Our England is a garden, and such gardens are not made by singing
– "Oh, how beautiful!", and sitting in the shade.'
Rudyard Kipling (1865–1936)

57: HERB REBUS
- Angelica

58: CANTERBURY TALES
- The Prioress
- The Reeve
- The Squire

59: PAIRING UP
- Common Butterwort – *Pinguicula vulgaris*
- Forked-leaved Sundew – *Drosera binata*
- Hooded Pitcher Plant – *Darlingtonia californica*
- Purple Pitcher Plant – *Sarracenia purpurea*
- Venus Fly Trap – *Dionaea muscipula*
- Yellow Trumpet – *Sarracenia flava*

60: GARDENING PROVERB
Germany

61: FLOWERS IN SONGS
'Roses are shining in Picardy,
In the hush of the silvery dew.'
Frederick Edward Weatherly (1848–1929)

62: WHICH FRUIT?

• Gooseberry

63: GARDENING PROVERB

'Love is not like a potato. You cannot throw it out of a window.'
Russian proverb

64: HERBACEOUS REBUS

• Acanthus

65: MOON SEED-SOWING

'Sow peasen and beans in the wane of the moon,
Who soweth them sooner, he soweth too soon,
That they with the planet may rest and arise,
And flourish with bearing most plentiful wise.'

66: MAKING HAY!

'A wet May makes loads of hay.'

67: SPOT THE DIFFERENCE

68: PAIRING UP
- Chinese Honeysuckle – *Lonicera nitida*
- Holly – *Ilex aquifolium*
- Lavender – *Lavandula angustifolia*
- Privet – *Ligustrum ovalifolium*
- Yew – *Taxus baccata*

69: ENTICING BEES
- Balm

70: HITCHING A LIFT!
- *Senecio squalidus* (Oxford Ragwort)

71: FRITILLARIA CONUNDRUM
- *Fritillaria imperialis*

72: MEMORABLE VERSE
''Tis the last rose of summer,
Left blooming alone;
All her lovely companions
Are faded and gone.'

73: VICAR'S SEED-SOWING ADVICE
'When the parson begins to read Genesis,
It's time to sow black oats.'

74: GARDENS IN LITERATURE
'God Almighty first planted a garden. And indeed it is the purest of
human pleasures.'
Francis Bacon (1561–1626)

75: COTTAGE GARDEN REBUS
- Hollyhock

76: SEED-SOWING PREDICTIONS

'Sow pease (good Trull),
The moon is past full,
Fine seeds then sow,
Whilst moon doth grow.'

77: FLOWER REBUS

• Snapdragon

78: FRENCHMAN'S DARLING

The flower is *Reseda odorata* (Mignonette), which was known as Frenchman's Darling on account of the claim that good fortune attends a lover who rolls three times in a bed of this flower.

79: STREWING FLOWERS FOR WEDDINGS

A combination of wild flowers, rushes and a scattering of wheat.

80: BENEFICIAL INSECT WORDSEARCH

81: KISSING RHYME
'When gorse is out of bloom,
Kissing's out of season.'
(Fortunately, gorse flowers throughout most of the year!)

82: WHISKERS ON HORSES
• Common Gorse

83: FLOWERS IN LITERATURE
'I wandered lonely as a cloud,
That floats on high o'er vales and hills,
When all at once I saw a crowd,
A host of golden daffodils.'
William Wordsworth (1770–1850)

84: WEATHER FORECASTING
'If the oak's before the ash,
You will only get a splash,
But if the ash precedes the oak,
You will surely get a soak.'

85: GODS, PATRONS, BADGES AND SYMBOLS
1. The Pomegranate Badge of Katherine of Aragon.
2. Shalako Mana, the Corn Mist Maiden of the Hopi Indians.
3. Cinteotl, the Maize God of the Mayan Indians.
4. The Mayan Rain God Smoking a
Cloud-blowing Pipe, Palenque, Mexico.
5. Inari, the Rice Bearer, from an old Japanese engraving.
6. Maize Symbol of the Pueblo Indians.
7. Aztec Maize Symbol of Fertility, Veracruz.

86: PROTECTING CARROTS
All three solutions will help to keep your carrots safe.

87: FLOWERS IN LITERATURE
'And I will make thee beds of roses,
And a thousand fragrant posies.'
Christopher Marlowe (1564–1593)

88: HERBACEOUS REBUS
- St Bernard's Lily

89: FEMALE FERTILITY
It was thought that because Tansy was often abundant where there were lots of rabbits it would be just as effective for women.

90: EBBS AND FLOWS!
'If it raineth when it doth flow,
Then yoke your ox and go to plough,
But if it raineth when it doth ebb,
Unyoke your ox and goe to bed.'

91: HARVESTING TIME
'If the moon shows a silver shield,
Be not afraid to reap your field,
But if she rises haloed round,
Soon we'll tread on deluged ground.'

92: HARVESTING APPLES
'Till St Swithin's day be past,
The apples be not fit to taste.'
(St Swithin's Day is 15 July)

93: GRAFTING AND PRUNING RHYME
'From moon being changed,
Till past be the prime,
For grafting and cropping,
Is very good time.'

94: SLUG AND SNAIL REPELLENTS
All four of these plants provide slug and snail protection.

95: PLANT HERALDRY
- England – Rose
- Ireland – Shamrock
- Scotland – Thistle
- Wales – Leek

96: SPOT THE DIFFERENCE

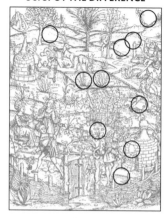

97: FIERY FLOWER
• *Eschscholzia californica*

98: LILY CONUNDRUM
• *Lilium auratum* – Golden-rayed Lily of Japan
• *Lilium candidum* – Madonna Lily
• *Lilium chalcedonicum* – Scarlet Turk's Cap Lily
• *Lilium pardalinum* – Leopard Lily
• *Lilium tigrinum* – Tiger Lily

99: GARDENING PROVERB
'Let your prayers for a good crop be short – and your hoeing be long.'
Albanian proverb

100: WHO'S IN CHARGE?
• Rosemary

101: LOVE APPLES
• Tomatoes

102: TOOTHACHE CURE
• Clove

103: KENDAL GREEN
• *Genista tinctoria* (Dyer's Greenweed)
• *Isatis tinctoria* (Dyer's Woad)

104: FIRE PROTECTION
• Houseleek

105: APPLE SPIDERMITE CROSSWORD

| B | R | A | M | L | E | Y | S | | S | E | E | D | L | I | N | G |
| | | | | | | | | | G | | | | | | | |

```
B R A M L E Y S   S E E D L I N G        D E L I C I O U S
                            R             I
      J A M E S   G R I E V E            S U N S E T
                            N            C
                            A        O R L E A N S   R E I N E T T E
K I D D S   O R A N G E   R E D          V
                            I            E
      G E O R G E   C A V E              R I B S T O N   P I P P I N
                            R            Y
```

106: FORAGING NIBBLE
• Fat Hen

107: PAIRING UP
• *Wisteria floribunda* – Japanese Wisteria
• *Wisteria frutescens* – American Wisteria
• *Wisteria sinensis* – Chinese Wisteria

108: CACTUS REBUS
• Rat's Tail Cactus

109: EVENING AND NIGHT SCENTS
- *Hesperis matronalis*
- *Matthiola longipetala* (*M. bicornis*)
- *Mirabilis jalapa*
- *Oenothera biennis*

110: WATERLILY JUMBLEY
- *Nymphaea*

111: GARDENING PROVERB
'When God blesses the harvest there is enough for the thief as well as the gardener.'
Polish proverb

112: FLOWERS IN LITERATURE
'She wore a wreath of roses
The night that first we met;
Her lovely face was smiling
Beneath her curls of jet.
Her footsteps had the lightness,
Her voice the joyous tone,
The tokens of a youthful heart,
Where sorrow is unknown,
I saw her but a moment,
Yet methinks I see her now,
With the wreath of summer flowers
Upon her snowy brow.'
She Wore a Wreath of Roses, Thomas Haynes Bayly (1797–1839)

113: TREE REBUS
- Strawberry Tree

114: FORAGING JUMBLEY
- Jack-in-the-Hedge

115: FRUIT JUMBLEY
• Cox's Orange Pippin

116: PLANTING RHYME
'When you hear the cuckoo shout,
'Tis time to plant your tatties out.'

117: ROSE PERFECTION
• Paris

118: PLAGUE ANTIDOTE
• Rue

119: SEED-SOWING PREDICTIONS
'When the elm leaf is as big as a mouse's ear,
Then to sow barley, never fear.'

120: ARM BLISTERER
• *Clematis vitalba* (Traveller's Joy)

121: PEAR VARIETY WORDSEARCH

P	A	M	F	Y	J	U	A	E	D	N	O	R	U	D
A	X	W	D	F	K	N	E	G	F	K	L	S	B	O
C	S	V	B	K	H	D	L	U	Y	T	X	E	Y	Y
K	A	N	J	Z	J	A	R	G	O	N	E	L	L	E
H	X	T	H	O	M	P	S	O	N	S	N	B	R	N
A	B	E	U	R	R	E	S	U	P	E	R	F	I	N
M	C	R	Y	D	R	A	H	E	R	R	U	E	B	E
S	O	N	W	A	R	D	Q	K	C	K	J	L	T	D
T	Y	E	K	R	B	T	N	L	T	K	I	H	V	U
R	L	L	H	E	B	E	T	H	Q	H	L	I	T	C
I	Z	I	V	T	Q	D	V	P	K	Q	V	E	Y	O
U	L	S	C	E	D	I	R	P	N	O	T	R	E	M
M	A	H	R	O	G	K	H	G	T	H	T	N	V	I
P	A	I	H	T	E	C	N	E	R	E	F	N	O	C
H	S	I	B	H	Q	Q	C	O	N	C	O	R	D	E

122: WHIN, GORSE OR FURZE?
- Furze – In the south
- Gorse – In the north
- Whin – In the east

123: DYING OF LAUGHTER
- Saffron Crocus

124: CAT'S DELIGHT
'If you set [plant] it, the cats will get it,
If you sow it, the cats won't know it.'

125: FLOWERS IN SONGS
'Tiptoe through the tulips with me.'
Lyrics: Al Dubin (1891–1945)
Music: Joe Burke (1884–1950)

126: MAGICAL SHRUB
This tree gains its name Witch Hazel from the apparent near-magical ability of its branches, when used as water-divining rods, to find water.

127: DETERRING MOLES
- *Euphorbia lathyris* (Caper Spurge)

128: FOOLING GREENFLY
- *Tagetes patula* (French Marigold)

129: SUNDIAL INSCRIPTION
'Time wastes our bodies and our wits,
But we waste Time, so we are quits.'

130: ENDURING THYME
'I know a bank whereon the wild thyme blows,
Where oxlips and the nodding violet grows,
Quite over-canopied with luscious woodbine,

With sweet musk-roses, and with eglantine.
There sleeps Titania some time of the night,
Lulled in these flowers with dances and delight.'
A Midsummer Night's Dream, William Shakespeare (1564–1616)

131: JAILHOUSE BLUES!
- Rue
- Southernwood

132: STRONGLY SCENTED
- Rosemary

133: JERSEY LILY
- *Amaryllis belladonna*

134: SHRIEKING PLANT
- *Mandragora officinarum* (Mandrake)

135: FRENCH CONNECTION
- *Artemisia abrotanum* (Southernwood)

136: WART FOLKLORE
'Ashen tree, Ashen tree,
Pray buy these warts off me.'

137: TEASING PLANT
- Fuller's Teasel

138: FASHIONS IN FLOWERS
1. Lotus – Ancient Egypt and India
2. Violet – Athens, 400 BC; Europe, 1790–1830, 1870–1914
3. Rose – Imperial Rome; Europe, 1800 and 20th century
4. Wallflower and Rosemary – Middle Ages
(especially during the Age of Chivalry)
5. Lily – Adored in France under Louis XII (1483–1515)
6. *Mirabilis jalapa* (Marvel of Peru) – Europe, 17th century

7. Fritillary – Germany, 16th and 17th centuries
8. Tulip – Holland, 1634–37; France, 1610; Turkey, 18th century
9. Hyacinth – Holland, 1637 to about 1700;
Germany, late 19th century
10. Auricula – England, 1730
11. *Bellis perennis* (Double Daisy) – 1750
12. Ranunculus – England, 18th century
13. Carnation – England, 1650; 1800; 20th century
14. Forget-me-not – France, 1800 (as a pot plant)
15. Dahlia – France, 1838; England, 1841; 20th century
16. Fuchsia – Berlin, 1830–40
17. Camellia – France, 1840 and 1860
18. Mignonette – 1810–1890 (as a pot plant)
19. White lilac – 1890–1900, and up to the 1940s
20. Pansy – 1870
(These are the times when the above plants were most popular, but many continued to be grown by garden enthusiasts and admirers.)

139: PAIRING UP
- Blue Beard – *Caryopteris × clandonensis*
- Butterfly Bush – *Buddleja davidii*
- Ice Plant – *Sedum spectabile*
- Michaelmas Daisy – *Aster novi-belgii*
- Sweet William – *Dianthus barbatus*

140: LOVING SIGNALS
- Red Hibiscus

141: DRUNKEN BLISS!
- Sugar and beer

142: PAIRING UP
- Black-stemmed Bamboo – *Phyllostachys nigra*
- Golden Bamboo – *Phyllostachys aurea*
- Square-stemmed Bamboo – *Chimonobambusa quadrangularis*

143: PROTECTING ROSES

Plant several clusters of chives around them, positioning them close to the border's edge so that you can cut the leaves for culinary purposes.

144: PAIRING UP

- Chickweed – *Stellaria media*
- Dandelion – *Taraxacum officinale*
- Field Bindweed – *Convolvulus arvensis*
- Ground Elder – *Aegopodium podagraria*
- Stinging Nettle – *Urtica dioica*
- Woodruff – *Galium odoratum*

145: HOUSEPLANT SPIDERMITE CROSSWORD

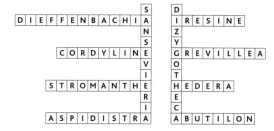

146: PAIRING UP

- *Aristolochia macrophylla* – Manure
- *Fritillaria imperialis* – Foxy
- *Lysichiton americanus* – Carrion and garlic
- *Lysichiton camtschatcensis* – Animal
- *Trillium erectum* – Putrid

147: BULB JUMBLEY

- *Chionodoxa*

148: KEEPING BEES AT BAY

- Asparagus

149: BEAUTIFUL ITALIAN LADIES
• Deadly Nightshade

150: VERSATILE NATIVE PLANT
• Dandelion

151: VEGETABLE RHYME
'I always eat peas with honey,
I've done it all my life,
They do taste kind of funny,
But it keeps them on the knife.'

152: PAIRING UP
• *Philodendron bipennifolium* – Fiddle-leaf Philodendron
• *Philodendron bipinnatifidum* – Tree Philodendron
• *Philodendron domesticum* – Elephant's Ear Philodendron
• *Philodendron erubescens* – Blushing Philodendron
• *Philodendron scandens* – Sweetheart Plant

153: PUBLICISING CUCUMBERS!
'A cucumber should be well sliced, and dressed with pepper
and vinegar, and then thrown out, as good for nothing.'

154: APOTHECARY'S ROSE
• *Rosa gallica* 'Officinalis'

155: DUTCH DUO
• The Early Dutch Honeysuckle – *Lonicera periclymenum* 'Belgica'
• The Late Dutch Honeysuckle – *Lonicera periclymenum* 'Serotina'

156: VIOLET-SCENTED ROOTS
• Orris Root

157: OPIUM POPPY
• *Papaver somniferum*

158: WEATHER RHYME

'If the cock moults before the hen,
We shall have weather thick and thin;
But if the hen moults before the cock,
We shall have weather hard as a block.'

159: PAIRING UP

- Christmas Rose – *Helleborus niger*
- Easter Lily – *Lilium longiflorum*
- Michaelmas Daisy – *Aster novi-belgii*
- Winter Jasmine – *Jasminum nudiflorum*
- Winter Sweet – *Chimonanthus praecox*

160: PAIRING UP

- *Hedera canariensis* – Canary Island Ivy
- *Hedera colchica* – Persian Ivy
- *Hedera helix* – Common Ivy
- *Hedera hibernica* – Irish Ivy

161: PAIRING UP

- *Chimonanthus praecox* – Winter Sweet
- *Daphne mezereum* – Mezereon
- *Hamamelis japonica* – Japanese Witch Hazel
- *Hamamelis mollis* – Chinese Witch Hazel
- *Hamamelis vernalis* – Ozark Witch Hazel

162: STRAWBERRY VARIETY WORDSEARCH

B	A	R	O	N	S	O	L	E	M	A	C	H	E	R
S	L	O	F	N	O	L	L	A	T	N	A	T	E	E
Z	E	Y	A	S	X	L	H	W	O	H	M	O	D	D
S	X	A	P	Z	A	S	A	L	S	X	B	T	N	G
P	A	L	L	F	L	H	R	E	T	H	R	E	A	A
W	N	S	H	S	L	P	V	M	A	X	I	M	R	U
F	D	O	G	R	E	X	E	O	R	H	D	W	G	N
W	R	V	E	O	U	S	S	R	A	P	G	Z	J	T
P	I	E	N	D	R	A	T	A	S	L	E	L	S	L
X	A	R	T	A	G	R	E	R	A	W	V	F	D	E
A	P	E	O	B	A	I	R	O	A	R	I	N	E	T
V	W	I	H	U	T	V	Z	D	L	H	G	K	L	Z
L	A	G	P	O	N	L	I	N	A	M	O	D	S	D
E	J	N	L	R	A	E	S	A	W	L	U	F	S	H
S	P	F	S	T	P	H	Z	P	S	C	R	D	J	F

163: PAIRING UP

- *Ficus benghalensis* – Bengal Fig
- *Ficus benjamina* – Weeping Fig
- *Ficus deltoidea* – Mistletoe Fig
- *Ficus elastica* – Rubber Plant
- *Ficus pumila* – Creeping Fig
- *Ficus religiosa* – Bo Tree

164: ADDING SPICINESS

- Clove Gilloflower

165: YUCCAS IN PRINT

- *The Daily Telegraph*

166: PIPE DREAM

- *Erica arborea*

167: PAIRING UP
- *Aloysia citrodora* – Lemon Verbena
- *Calycanthus floridus* – Carolina Allspice
- *Choisya ternata* – Mexican Orange Blossom
- *Cistus ladanifer* – Gum Cistus
- *Rosmarinus officinalis* – Rosemary

168: VEGETABLE REBUS
- Potatoes

169: VEGETABLE JUMBLEY
- Scorzonera

170: A BOUNTY ON THIS FOOD!
- Breadfruit

171: EARLY DIGGING AND PLOUGHING TOOLS
1. Trenching gouge also used as a spade
2. Turving space
3. Paring spade
4. Trenching spade
5. Plain trenching plough
6. Wheeled trenching plough
7. Trenching spade cutting a trench, with water following it
8. Single-wheeled plough

172: PAIRING UP
- *Jasminum humile* – Italian Yellow Jasmine
- *Jasminum mesnyi* – Primrose Jasmine
- *Jasminum nudiflorum* – Winter-flowering Jasmine
- *Jasminum officinale* – Common White Jasmine
- *Jasminum polyanthum* – Pink Jasmine

173: FRUIT JUMBLEY
- Black Hamburgh

174: BRIDESMAID'S DELIGHT
- *Achillea ptarmica*

175: PAIRING UP
- *Mentha × gracilis* – Ginger Mint
- *Mentha × piperita* – Peppermint
- *Mentha spicata* – Spearmint
- *Mentha suaveolens* – Applemint
- *Mentha suaveolens* 'Variegata' – Pineapple Mint

176: BUTCHER'S BROOM
- *Ruscus aculeatus*

177: SHRUB REBUS
- Camellia

178: AMERICAN SUNDIAL INSCRIPTION
'Hours fly,
Flowers die
New days,
New ways,
Pass by;
Love stays.'

179: PAIRING UP
- *Acorus calamus* – Camphor
- *Geum rivale* – Beer
- *Glycyrrhiza glabra* – Liquorice
- *Iris florentina* – Violets
- *Rhodiola rosea* – Rose

180: FRUIT JUMBLEY
- Pomegranate

181: PAIRING UP
- Common Horsetail – *Equisetum arvense*
- Couch Grass – *Agropyron repens*
- Field Bindweed – *Convolvulus arvensis*
- Ground Elder – *Aegopodium podagraria*
- Lesser Celandine – *Ranunculus ficaria*

182: VEGETABLE WORDSEARCH

B	X	H	C	R	N	M	C	A	B	B	A	G	E	L
F	R	E	N	C	H	B	E	A	N	S	X	V	X	E
S	U	U	Q	X	K	S	L	S	V	N	K	L	A	E
S	N	E	S	S	W	E	E	T	C	O	R	N	S	K
T	N	C	K	S	D	K	R	L	X	I	X	K	P	S
O	E	U	L	V	E	W	Y	D	Q	N	J	W	A	B
R	R	T	C	A	U	L	I	F	L	O	W	E	R	R
R	B	T	Q	P	A	R	S	N	I	P	S	L	A	O
A	E	E	X	S	W	K	V	S	J	L	E	Q	G	A
C	A	L	A	B	R	E	S	E	P	D	J	A	U	D
V	N	W	S	I	L	O	C	C	O	R	B	J	S	B
Q	S	X	S	E	T	T	E	G	R	U	O	C	W	E
T	O	M	A	T	O	E	S	P	I	N	R	U	T	A
W	O	R	R	A	M	B	E	E	T	R	O	O	T	N
G	L	O	B	E	A	R	T	I	C	H	O	K	E	S

183: PAIRING UP

- *Chionodoxa* – Glory of the Snow
- *Galanthus* – Snowdrop
- *Leucojum* – Snowflake

184: VEGETABLE JUMBLEY

- Chicory

185: IRISH MOSS JUMBLEY

- Carrageen

186: PERIWINKLE APHRODISIAC

- Nicholas Culpeper (1616–1654)

187: BENEFICIAL GARDEN CREATURES WORDSEARCH

S	H	Z	G	U	S	J	T	S	V
L	E	J	U	S	E	Ø	Q	E	K
O	D	D	V	P	A	S	V	P	J
W	G	Q	E	Ø	K	G	S	G	V
W	E	V	S	P	I	D	E	R	S
O	H	S	G	H	I	G	K	U	Z
R	O	F	O	Z	R	T	U	G	K
M	G	V	R	G	U	E	N	S	V
S	S	K	F	K	S	U	W	E	U
G	Z	G	V	Z	V	G	Q	S	C

188: BRIGHTENING WAYSIDE HEDGES
- Old Man's Beard
- Traveller's Joy

189: FRUIT REBUS
- Bullace

190: VEGETABLE JUMBLEY
- Good King Henry

193: COASTAL FOOD JUMBLEY
- Laver

194: BEAUX BEWARE!
'Ivy, Ivy, I love you,
In my bosom I put you,
The first young man who speaks to me
My future husband he will be.'

195: COCKROACH DETERRENT
- *Verbascum blattaria* (Moth Mullein)

194: FLOWERING HOUSEPLANT WORDSEARCH

```
P A C H Y S T A C H Y S J S E
S N E R L G J K C S Q L X I O
K Y M L A C A A Z A K Y B T H
B H R U L S L R I L T A O C
B U A E L I S D C A Y Z N N
E R R Z P L V I A E S K R A A
N I D B C T Y N F N N I A H L
O U N K B O O H I L T I R P A
R M A S X S L C R A O H A E K
E A L S K Z T U A G R U T Z
P B E G O N I A M R H U A S A
O S H C U P H E A N R T O A L
L L P L U M B A G O E U A B J
E T A I L U A P T N I A S R B
B O U V A R D I A X J Z L J S
```

195: BIRD OMENS

'The robin and the red-breast,
The martin and the swallow,
If ye touch one o' their eggs,
Ill luck will surely follow.'

196: CHURCH TITHES

'We've cheated the Parson, we'll cheat him again,
Why should the vicar have one in ten?
One in ten, one in ten,
Why should the Vicar have one in ten?'

197: PROTECTING SEEDS
• Gorse

198: FOOT-ROT CURE!
• Alder

199: VERSATILE CULINARY HERB
• Caraway

ABOUT DAVID SQUIRE

David Squire studied horticulture and botany at the Hertfordshire College of Horticulture and The Royal Horticultural Society's Garden at Wisley, Surrey, where he gained the Wisley Diploma in Horticulture. A career in magazine journalism followed, with spells on *The Home Gardener* magazine and *Garden News*. David is now a freelance author and has written over 80 books which have been sold in more than 18 countries. He has contributed to several gardening part-works. David has a special interest in scented plants and one of his books, *The Scented Garden*, won the Garden Writers of America Quill and Trowel Award. He has also written several books about dogs and hens, as well as having a passion for plant folklore and garden history.

If you're interested in finding out more about our books,
find us on Facebook at **Summersdale Publishers** and
follow us on Twitter at **@Summersdale**.

WWW.SUMMERSDALE.COM